Happy Birthday
Jane.

This Book Belongs to

Ms. Harini

Bajaj

The mission of Storey Communications is to serve our customers
by publishing practical information that encourages personal independence
in harmony with the environment.

Edited by Pamela Lappies
Cover and interior illustrations by Mary Rich
Design and production by Meredith Maker
Production assistance by Susan Bernier
Indexed by Northwind Editorial Services

Some recipes have been adapted from other Storey Publishing books: pages 6, 56: *At Home with Herbs* by Jane Newdick; page 8: A-40 *Mushroom Cookery* by Jo Mueller; page 10: *Tomatoes! 365 Healthy Recipes for Year-Round Enjoyment* by the Editors of Garden Way Publishing; page 14: *Picnic!* by Edith Stovel; pages 18, 26: *Herbal Treasures* by Phyllis V. Shaudys; pages 20, 28, 58, 60: *Herbs for Weddings and Other Celebrations* by Bertha Reppert; page 46: *Broccoli & Company* by Audra and Jack Hendrickson; pages 48, 49: *Making and Using Flavored Vinegars* by Glenn Andrews; pages 50, 52: *The Joy of Gardening Cookbook* by Janet Ballantyne.

Copyright © 1996 Storey Communications, Inc.

The information in this book is true and complete to the best of our knowledge. All recommendations are made without guarantee on the part of the author or Storey Communications, Inc. The author and publisher disclaim any liability in connection with the use of this information. For additional information please contact Storey Communications, Inc., Schoolhouse Road, Pownal, Vermont 05261.

Printed in Canada by Métropole Litho

10 9 8 7 6 5 4 3 2 1

**Library of Congress
Cataloging-in-Publication Data**

Bass, Ruth, 1934–
    Herbal Salads / Ruth Bass
        p.   cm.
    "A fresh-from-the-garden cookbook."
    "A Storey Publishing Book."
    ISBN 0-88266-925-7 (hc : alk. paper)
    1. Cookery (Herbs)   2. Salads.
    I. Title.
TX819.H4B385 1996
641.8'3—dc20   96-1717
                                            CIP

HeRBAL SaLADs

A
Fresh from the Garden
Cookbook

RUTH BASS

ILLUSTRATED BY MARY RICH

A Storey Publishing Book
Storey Communications, Inc.

Introduction

Herb gardens in books frequently look as if they began with a designer and continued with a professional gardener — someone who comes daily to pull weeds, sweep miniature stone pathways, and possibly dust the leaves of the basil and Italian parsley. But ordinary people have herb gardens, too, or herbs among the tomatoes, beans, and zucchinis. Many herbs are easy to grow.

Cooks in areas where frost comes late in spring and early in fall will reap a better harvest by starting with greenhouse-grown plants rather than seeds. If you've taken the trouble to grow flavor in your garden and you live in a climate where September and October bring hard frost, you'll be sad to see the basil turn black, the dill wilt, and the other herbs fade and disappear. But you don't have to go without. Before frost, save some of your herbs and take their freshness into the kitchen. The easiest way is to pick them, preferably before they blossom, tie a number of long sprigs together and hang the lot upside down in a well-ventilated place. If you put the bundles inside a brown paper bag, you'll conquer the dust problem. The only remaining dilemma is whether to explain the bags hanging from your ceiling — or let visitors wonder.

When the herbs are dry, remove the stems — either shake the bag or run your thumb and forefinger along each stem. Pour into glass jars, label, and store with your other herbs.

You can also grow fresh herbs indoors. One of the best and most decorative ways is to plant an herb dish garden. Houseplant expert Shirl Fowler of Lenox,

Massachusetts, writes that an 18-inch shallow clay bowl, perforated for drainage and set on a platter or large plate — a large pizza pan might be just the thing — will hold a variety of herbs, providing both a source of good flavors and a conversation piece.

"You certainly can use them," Shirl says. "The more they are snipped, the better they grow." She advises embedding some rocks in the potting soil mix to create a landscape and then treating the whole thing like a terrarium. If it will be viewed from all sides, plant tall herbs in the middle, shorter ones around them, creeping ones on the outside.

You'll need to visit a good herb shop or herb-oriented nursery to get your plants going — and be sure to ask if they've been sprayed, so you'll know whether they need a scrubbing or not.

If you have neither a garden in summer nor a green thumb, then have a look at what's happened in supermarkets. Where once the tired parsley drooped alone, a grand variety of appealing fresh herbs is now sold in bulk or in plastic envelopes that give you a small quantity of fresh rosemary, sage, lemon balm, chervil, cilantro, mint — you name it.

If all else fails, you can buy dried herbs. They may be dried, grayish-green, and innocuous looking, but in most recipes, you should use only half as much of the herb if it's dried. Sometimes a three to one ratio is even better. Store them in a dry place, never in sunshine, in containers with tight covers, and clean out the herb shelves the same way you clean out the medicine cabinet. Old herbs are as ineffective as old pills.

Roasted Pepper, Garlic, and Basil Salad

Peppers turn mellow and glossy under the broiler and melt in your mouth. This salad could be a handsome appetizer or a room-temperature vegetable served with the main course.

>   4 *green bell peppers*
>   4 *red, yellow, or orange bell peppers*
>   4 *garlic cloves, minced*
>   1 *tablespoon top quality olive oil*
>   ¼ *cup red wine vinegar*
>   A *bunch of basil*

1. Preheat the broiler and place the whole peppers on a broiler pan. Broil under high heat, turning frequently, for about 5 minutes or until the peppers are wrinkled. The peppers can also be cooked on an outdoor grill.
2. Wrap the peppers loosely in plastic and let them cool.
3. Remove the plastic wrap. Remove the skin from the peppers — it should come off easily. Slice the peppers in narrow strips, removing the core, stalk, and seeds. Arrange the strips on a flat serving platter.
4. Mix the garlic with the oil and vinegar. Sprinkle over the peppers.
5. Slice the basil leaves into long strips and scatter over the peppers. Marinate for an hour or so at room temperature. Do not chill.

4–6 SERVINGS

Garlic's flavor is more intense when grown in hotter climates.

Fresh Mushroom, Parsley, and Radish Salad

Raw mushrooms are a real treat — smooth textured with a woodsy taste that is like nothing else in a salad dressing. This salad adds radishes for color and sharpness.

> 1 garlic clove, pressed
> 8 large white mushrooms, thinly sliced
> ⅓ cup minced fresh parsley
> 2 tablespoons lemon juice
> ⅓ cup extra virgin olive oil
> Pinch of chopped fresh basil leaves
> Salt and freshly ground pepper
> 6 cups mixed salad greens: arugula, chicory,
>   oak leaf lettuce, Bibb lettuce
> ⅓ cup finely chopped radishes

1. Place the garlic, mushrooms, parsley, lemon juice, and oil in a glass bowl and toss with the basil. Salt and pepper to taste. Marinate at least 30 minutes.
2. Add the greens and toss. Sprinkle with the radishes and serve.

2 MAIN-DISH SERVINGS

Milt's Tomatoes with Mozzarella

Quick to prepare, appealing to the eye, and in harmony with a summer day — what more could anyone want from a simple salad? You will need really ripe red tomatoes for the best effect. If you use a serrated tomato knife, you'll be sure of getting uniform, unsquashed slices.

2 giant tomatoes, sliced not more than
¼-inch thick
¼ pound fresh mozzarella, thinly sliced
4 or 5 basil leaves, chopped
Freshly ground pepper
Extra virgin olive oil

1. Arrange the tomato and mozzarella slices on a black, white, or glass plate.
2. Scatter the basil over the top. Grind a generous amount of fresh pepper over the basil, and dot the tomatoes with the oil.
3. Chill if made ahead of time, but bring almost to room temperature before serving.

4 SERVINGS

Sun-dried Tomatoes and Rotini

The juiciness of fresh tomatoes combines with the piquant flavor of their sun-dried cousins to create an appealing salad that can be an appetizer or part of the main course. Other pasta shapes can be tried, and buying shredded mozzarella will cut a little off the 20-minute preparation time.

½ cup olive oil
2 tablespoons red wine vinegar
2 garlic cloves, minced
Salt and freshly ground pepper
4 medium tomatoes, chopped (about 2 cups)
12 sun-dried tomatoes
12 ounces low-fat fresh mozzarella cheese, cut
   in ¼-inch cubes
4 tablespoons chopped fresh basil leaves
4 cups cooked rotini pasta

1. In a large bowl, combine the oil, vinegar, garlic, salt and pepper to taste, and tomatoes.
2. Add the sun-dried tomatoes, cheese, basil, and pasta.
3. Toss to blend and chill for an hour.

6–8 SERVINGS

Basil represents good wishes.

Fusilli Avocado Salad

Pop a crusty loaf of bread in the oven, put this salad together, and you have a meal that's perfect for the two-career couple. If you've forgotten to pick up any of the ingredients, substitute what you do have or leave it out. It will be good anyway.

SALAD

½ pound fusilli pasta
1 head loose leaf lettuce, red or green
1 ripe dark-skinned avocado, peeled
¼ pound sharp cheddar cheese
2 medium tomatoes
1 cucumber, peeled
1 bunch fresh broccoli (or 10 ounces frozen), cooked
1 onion, chopped
¼ pound sliced turkey or chicken

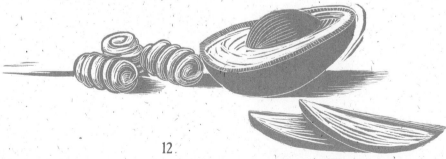

DRESSING

- 2 tablespoons red wine vinegar
- 2 tablespoons extra virgin olive oil
- 1 tablespoon chopped fresh basil leaves
- 1 tablespoon chopped fresh parsley
- 1 garlic clove, minced
- ¼ teaspoon dry mustard
- Freshly ground pepper
- ⅛ pound crumbled blue cheese (optional)

1. Cook the pasta according to package directions. Tear the lettuce into bite-size pieces. Cube the avocado, cheese, tomatoes, and cucumber. Chop the broccoli and onion. Cut the turkey or chicken into thin strips.
2. Toss the avocado, cheese, and vegetables with the turkey or chicken and the pasta.
3. Mix together the vinegar, oil, basil, parsley, garlic, mustard, pepper to taste, and blue cheese. Pour over the salad. Toss gently.

2 MAIN-DISH SERVINGS

Tortellini Salad with Pine Nuts

Tortellini salad with the added crunch of pine nuts is perfect for the picnic basket or the patio buffet. Sweet peppers, red and green, give it color. Basil and dill give it flavor.

SALAD

    2 *pounds fresh tortellini pasta*
    1 *large green pepper, seeded and chopped*
    1 *large red bell pepper, seeded and chopped*
    2 *bunches scallions, chopped, with some green tops*
  ½ *cup pine nuts, chopped*
  ¼ *cup chopped fresh basil leaves*
  ¼ *cup snipped fresh dill*
  ¼ *cup Parmesan cheese, grated*

DRESSING

  ¼ *cup balsamic vinegar*
  1 *garlic clove, minced*
  ¼ *teaspoon salt*
     Freshly ground black pepper
  ¾ *cup peanut oil*

1. In a large pot of rapidly boiling water, cook the tortellini until it is al dente. The amount of time this takes will depend on the tortellini. Drain and place in a large bowl.
2. Add the peppers, scallions, pine nuts, basil, dill, and cheese. Toss gently.
3. In a small bowl, combine the vinegar, garlic, salt, and pepper to taste. Whisk in the oil until well combined.
4. Pour the dressing over the tortellini and chill.

8 GENEROUS SERVINGS

Mercury claims dominion over savory.
Keep it dry by you all the year,
if you love yourself and your ease.

— *Nicholas Culpeper*

Jewel Coleslaw

Rich colors make coleslaw spectacular instead of humdrum in this simple recipe. The truly adventurous could use half red and half green sweet peppers for even more color.

1 *head purple cabbage*
1 *large white onion*
1 *large green pepper*
¾ *cup balsamic vinegar*
½ *cup corn oil*
¾ *cup sugar*
½ *teaspoon salt*
2 *teaspoons minced fresh savory*
1 *teaspoon celery seeds*

1. Using the shredding blade in a food processor, shred the cabbage, onion, and green pepper. Toss together in a glass or plain white salad bowl.
2. Bring the vinegar, oil, sugar, salt, savory, and celery seeds to a boil. Pour over the vegetables and chill well.

6–8 SERVINGS

Lemon Summer Salad

In season, when lettuce is fairly tumbling out of the bins in the produce section of the grocery store or at roadside stands, a salad can be a beautiful creation. That's Linda Morgan's intent at her Antique Orchid Herbary in Virginia where she makes this dressing. Vary the salad ingredients according to what is in season.

DRESSING

    Juice of 1 large lemon (about ¼ cup)
1½ teaspoons grated lemon peel
  1 small garlic clove, crushed
  1 teaspoon minced fresh thyme
  1 teaspoon minced fresh lemon thyme
1½ teaspoons sugar (more, if lemon is very tart)
  ¾ cup oil (blend safflower, olive, and vegetable oils)
  ½ teaspoon salt
    Freshly ground black pepper
  ⅓ cup finely chopped parsley

SALAD

A variety of fresh greens, freshly washed and dried
½ cup sorrel leaves
1 small cucumber, chopped
2 scallions, sliced in thin rings

1. To make the dressing, put the lemon juice, lemon peel, garlic, thyme, lemon thyme, sugar, oil, salt, and pepper to taste in a jar with a tight cover. Shake until the mixture is opaque. Refrigerate for at least 2 hours so the flavors will blend.

2. Gently tear the greens and place in a bowl. Add the sorrel leaves, cucumber, and scallions.

3. About a half hour before serving, add the parsley to the dressing and shake well before dressing the salad.

4–6 SERVINGS

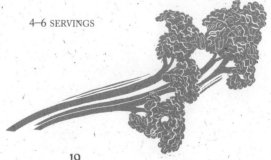

19

Salad Strata

One of the great things about this salad is that unlike most of its cousins it can be made a day ahead of time. The other great thing is that people like to eat it.

1 large head of lettuce
Several stalks of celery
2 medium green peppers
1 medium sweet onion
1 (10-ounce) package of frozen peas or sugar peas
1 cup sour cream or plain yogurt
1 cup mayonnaise, thinned with 2 tablespoons
    low-fat milk
2 tablespoons sugar
¼ pound cheddar or Monterey Jack cheese, grated
1 cup minced fresh herbs, choosing from parsley, mint,
    chervil, burnet, or lovage

1. Quarter, wash, drain, cut fine, and pat dry the lettuce. Wash and scrape the celery, and cut into small pieces. It should make about 2 cups. Wash, core, seed, and cut the peppers into strips. Slice the onion into paper-thin rings.
2. Cook the peas or sugar peas in a little salted water; rinse with cold water and drain.

3. Place the vegetables in layers in a glass bowl in the order listed, saving half of the lettuce to put on top of the other vegetables. Mix the sour cream (or yogurt) and mayonnaise together and spread over the salad. Do not stir.
4. Sprinkle the sugar over the salad and cover it with the grated cheese. Cover the bowl with plastic wrap and refrigerate for a minimum of 8 hours but preferably 24.

8 GENEROUS SERVINGS

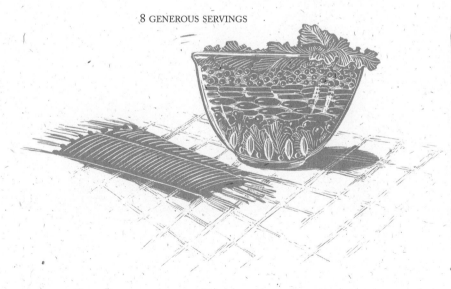

Kate's Fresh Salsa

Jars of salsa in varying degrees of hotness line the grocery shelves and challenge the shopper to make a decision. But once you have started making your own, you won't have to decide among them anymore. There's no going back. This recipe involves only 15 minutes of preparation time. Serve it with a mound of crisp tortilla chips — they even make them nonfat now — and watch it all disappear. Or serve as a first-course salad with warm flour tortillas that can be used to scoop up the salsa.

> 2 large tomatoes, chopped and seeded (about 1 cup)
> 1 medium Vidalia or sweet onion, chopped
> Juice of 1 lime (about 2 tablespoons)
> ⅓ cup chopped fresh cilantro
> 2 tablespoons chopped green chilies
> 2 drops Tabasco sauce
> Salt and freshly ground pepper

1. Mix the tomatoes, onion, lime juice, cilantro, chilies, and Tabasco in a medium-size bowl. Add salt and pepper to taste. If you make the salsa ahead of time, leave out the chilies until just before serving.
2. Let stand for 30 minutes to blend the flavors.

2 CUPS

Cilantro, also known as coriander,
is widely used in foods throughout the world.

Cacik

Pronounced "jah-jik," cacik is a Middle Eastern specialty made with lots of yogurt and dill. To vary the recipe, add ½ teaspoon of ground cumin to the yogurt mixture or increase the dill.

> 2 cups plain yogurt
> 1 tablespoon finely snipped fresh dill or 1 teaspoon
>   ground dried
> 2–3 large garlic cloves, chopped and crushed
> 1 medium cucumber, peeled and diced
> 3–4 parsley sprigs

1. Mix yogurt, dill, and garlic in a glass or ceramic bowl. Cover and refrigerate for at least 3 hours.
2. Gently stir in the cucumber pieces just before serving. Garnish with parsley sprigs.

6–8 SERVINGS

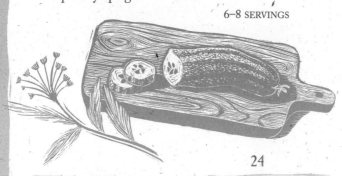

Herbed Vegetable Salad

For a colorful salad that you can make hours before dinnertime, try this melange of vegetables and fresh herbs.

5 cups carrots, green beans, cauliflower, and broccoli
    in any combination, cut into bite-size pieces
1 red onion, thinly sliced
½ cup salad oil
½ cup cider vinegar
2 tablespoons lemon juice
1 teaspoon each minced fresh oregano, basil,
    and rosemary
1 garlic clove, minced
½ cup minced fresh parsley

1. Cook the carrots, green beans, cauliflower, and broccoli until tender but not soft. Drain, place in a bowl, and toss gently.
2. Separate the onion slices into rings and arrange on top of the other vegetables.
3. Blend the oil, vinegar, lemon juice, oregano, basil, rosemary, garlic, and parsley and pour over the vegetables. Chill for several hours.

6–8 SERVINGS

Shrimp Dill Salad

The sweetness of raspberry vinegar, the richness of ripe avocados, and the bite of shallots, garlic, and mustard create a winning combination in this attractive summer salad.

2 tablespoons chopped shallots
6 garlic cloves, chopped (about 1 tablespoon)
1 tablespoon Dijon mustard
1 tablespoon honey
1 tablespoon raspberry vinegar
1 tablespoon red wine vinegar
½ cup snipped fresh dill
1 tablespoon chopped fresh parsley
⅔ cup peanut oil
1 pound shrimp, cooked and peeled
1 head Boston lettuce, torn
2 ripe avocados, thinly sliced
2 tomatoes, thinly sliced

1. Mix the shallots, garlic, mustard, honey, vinegars, dill, parsley, and oil. Beat until well blended and pour over the shrimp. Allow to marinate 3 to 4 hours.
2. Remove the shrimp and arrange on lettuce leaves. Garnish with avocado and tomato slices.

4 SERVINGS

Chicken Salad in a Lily

If you have unsprayed day lilies in your garden, consider serving them stuffed with this chicken salad. The day lilies are not only lovely containers but edible ones. It is best to cook the chicken a day or two before preparing this elegant party fare.

BASIC CHICKEN SALAD

3-pound whole chicken
4 quarts water
½ cup chopped fresh parsley
4 tablespoons chopped sweet onion
2 teaspoons finely chopped fresh tarragon or 1 teaspoon dried
Pinch of dried rosemary
Pinch of fresh lemon thyme, burnet, or lovage
14–15 large celery stalks
4 cups mayonnaise
12 unsprayed day lilies

28

OPTIONAL INGREDIENTS
black olives
1 Red Delicious apple, diced
almonds, slivered
peanuts
mandarin oranges
diced roasted peppers
sliced water chestnuts

1. In a large soup pot, combine the chicken, water, parsley, onion, tarragon, rosemary, and whichever herb you are using. Chop 6 stalks of the celery and add to the pot. Cook until the chicken meat falls away from the bone, about 40 to 50 minutes. Cool.
2. Debone and skin the cooled chicken and cut into bite-size pieces until you have 4 cups. Reserve any extra chicken and the broth for another use. Mince the remaining celery. (You should have about 4 cups.)
3. Combine the chicken, celery, and mayonnaise. Add any of the optional ingredients, in any combination that suits your eye and taste buds.
4. Stuff the day lilies with the chicken salad just before serving.

12 SERVINGS

Fruited Chicken Salad

Grapes and chicken marry well. For the best results, take the time to slice the grapes in half. This dish is perfect for a summer lunch, the centerpiece of a picnic, or a cool supper.

2 large boned chicken breasts, cooked and
    cubed (about 4 cups)
2 celery stalks, chopped (about ¾ cup)
1 (11-ounce) can mandarin oranges, drained
1 cup seedless white grapes, halved
¼ cup mayonnaise
3 tablespoons low-fat milk
Juice of half a lemon
2 tablespoons finely chopped fresh parsley
Salt
2 teaspoons celery seed
2 teaspoons finely chopped fresh savory or 1 teaspoon dried
Bibb lettuce

1. Combine the chicken, celery, oranges, and grapes. Set aside.
2. Thin the mayonnaise with the milk and lemon juice. Add the parsley, salt to taste, celery seed, and savory. Mix well.
3. Combine the dressing with the chicken mixture and chill well. Serve cupped in leaves of Bibb lettuce.

6 SERVINGS

Greek Rice Salad

The starches — potatoes, pasta, and rice — make summer salads that can be served chilled or at room temperature for full flavor. While white rice will do, brown is recommended, not only for its nutritional value but also for its nutty taste.

> 1½ cups uncooked rice
> 2 cups water
> 2 tablespoons white vinegar
> 3½ tablespoons olive oil
> 1 teaspoon finely chopped fresh oregano, or
> ½ teaspoon dried
> ¼ cup finely chopped fresh parsley
> 1 garlic clove, minced or crushed
> Salt and freshly ground pepper
> 10–12 Greek olives, green and black, pitted
> and chopped
> 1 head Bibb lettuce, separated, or 12 ounces fresh
> spinach leaves
> ½ cup crumbled feta cheese

1. Cook the rice according to the package directions but without adding any flavorings or butter.

2. While the rice cooks, mix in a jar the water, vinegar, oil, oregano, parsley, garlic, and salt and pepper to taste. Cover and shake well.
3. Combine the cooked rice and chopped olives in a glass or ceramic bowl. Pour the dressing over the mixture and toss.
4. Arrange the cuplike leaves of the Bibb lettuce or the stemmed spinach leaves on 4 salad plates. Fill with the rice and olive mixture and sprinkle the feta cheese on top.

4 SERVINGS

Tabbouleh

Throughout the Middle East, this minty salad is made with many variations. The key ingredients, however, are the bulgur (cracked wheat), parsley, and mint, and the result is a refreshing and satisfying salad. This regional version adds ½ cup cooked, cooled peas.

½ cup bulgur
2 cups boiling water
½ cup peas
3 ripe tomatoes
1 cucumber, peeled
5 scallions
4 tablespoons olive oil
Juice of one lemon
1 large bunch mint (about 8 ounces), finely chopped
1 large bunch flat-leaf parsley (about 8 ounces), finely chopped
Salt and freshly ground pepper

1. Put the bulgur in a large bowl and pour the boiling water over it. Cover and let stand for at least 30 minutes, until all the water is absorbed.
2. Cook the peas until tender but not soft, about 4 minutes. Drain and set aside to cool.
3. Dice the tomatoes and cucumber into small pieces. Thinly slice the scallions and add to the tomatoes. Mix the oil and lemon juice.
4. Combine the bulgur with the peas and the tomato mixture and stir gently. Add the mint, parsley, and salt and pepper to taste and toss with the oil and lemon juice. Set in a cool place for about an hour so the flavor can develop.

6–8 SERVINGS

Marinated Potato Salad

Potato salad is such a traditional favorite that nearly every family loves a particular one. The potato being a pale, bland, yet wonderful vegetable, it occasionally needs new treatment. This variation is simple but tasty.

> 8 large potatoes, peeled
> 1 yellow onion, finely chopped
> 2 garlic cloves, minced
> 3 teaspoons minced fresh oregano
> 2 tablespoons olive oil
> 2 tablespoons cider vinegar
> ½ cup mayonnaise
> Salt and freshly ground pepper
> 3 hard-cooked eggs
> 4–6 frilly lettuce leaves
> Paprika and parsley sprigs for garnish

1. Cook the potatoes until tender but not soft. Cool, then cut into cubes.
2. Make a marinade by mixing the onion, garlic, and oregano with the oil and vinegar.

3. While the potatoes are still warm, pour the marinade over them and toss as gently as possible. Cover with plastic wrap and refrigerate.
4. Just before serving, mix in the mayonnaise and salt and pepper to taste. Chop the hard-cooked eggs and gently toss with the salad. Arrange on a bed of lettuce. Sprinkle paprika on top and tuck parsley sprigs around the edges for color.

4 SERVINGS

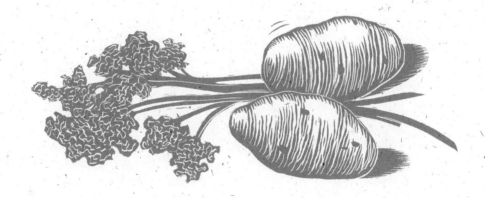

Yellow Beets and Green Bean Salad

For this dish you'll want freshly picked beans with plenty of life in them. It will take about 30 minutes to prepare this salad, including cooking the vegetables.

½ pound crisp green beans with the ends snipped
3 medium-size yellow beets, diced
1 teaspoon minced fresh tarragon
2 tablespoons chopped fresh parsley
5 ounces plain low-fat yogurt
1 tablespoon tahini (sesame seed paste)
1 tablespoon fresh lemon juice
1 garlic clove, crushed
Salt and freshly ground pepper

1. In a saucepan, cook the green beans in rapidly boiling water for 7 minutes or until they are tender but crisp. In a separate saucepan, cook the beets until they are tender. (You may cook both in the microwave according to your oven's instructions if you prefer.) Cool rapidly under cold running water and peel the beets.

2. Combine the beans with the beets, the tarragon, and half the parsley in a medium-size serving bowl. Mix well but gently.
3. In a small bowl, combine the yogurt, tahini, lemon juice, garlic, and salt and pepper to taste. Mix well. Stir the yogurt mixture into the green bean mixture and garnish with the remaining parsley. Serve immediately.

4 SERVINGS

Parsley is rich in vitamin C and iron.

Adriatic Bean Salad

Black beans need better publicity. They are an underrated source of nutrients and, combined with the sweet-and-sour taste of balsamic vinegar, they taste spectacular. Colorful peppers and bright parsley give the salad visual pizazz. For a little more bite, substitute cilantro for the parsley.

1 large yellow pepper
1 large green pepper
2 cups cooked black beans (or one 16-ounce can)
2 tablespoons coarsely chopped sweet onion
1 tablespoon balsamic vinegar
1 tablespoon olive oil
1½ tablespoons water
1 teaspoon minced fresh thyme
3 garlic cloves, minced
1 teaspoon minced fresh marjoram
Salt and freshly ground pepper
½ cup chopped fresh parsley

1. Chop the peppers, removing the seeds. In a bowl, combine the peppers with the beans. The beans should be warm.
2. In a small jar with a tight-fitting lid, combine the onion, vinegar, oil, water, thyme, garlic, marjoram, and salt and pepper to taste. Shake until they are combined. Pour over the bean mixture and toss gently.
3. Sprinkle the parsley over the top, cover with plastic wrap, and chill for a minimum of 2 hours.
4. Stir in the parsley just before serving.

4 SERVINGS

Oregano means "joy of the mountain."

Three Bean Salad

For color and for speed of preparation, it's hard to beat this salad, which is a great addition to any buffet.

>   2 cups cooked chick peas or 1 (16-ounce) can, drained
>   2 cups cooked red kidney beans or 1 (16-ounce)
>   can, drained
>   2 cups green beans, cooked until tender crisp or 1
>   (16-ounce) can, drained
>   1 sweet onion, peeled and sliced paper-thin
>   2–4 garlic cloves, minced
>   2 tablespoons finely chopped oregano
>   Salt and freshly ground pepper
>   ⅔ cup olive oil
>   ¼ cup vinegar

1. In a large bowl, combine the chick peas, kidney beans, green beans, and onion.
2. Mix the garlic, oregano, salt and pepper to taste, oil, and vinegar and pour over the bean mixture. Toss gently. Let stand at room temperature for at least 30 minutes. Serve warm or chilled.

8 SERVINGS

Green Bean Salad

When evenings are so warm that no one wants the stove turned on, and green beans are young and slender and crisp, prepare this recipe in the cool of the morning. The key to success here is marinating the fresh beans while they are still hot.

SALAD

3 teaspoons snipped fresh dill or an equal amount
   of chopped fresh oregano
½ cup olive oil
3 tablespoons white vinegar
1 tablespoon balsamic vinegar
1 pound fresh, young green beans
4–6 frilly lettuce leaves

SUGGESTED GARNISHES
hard-cooked egg
red bell pepper
Greek olives
tomato

1. Mix the dill or oregano, oil, and vinegars.
2. Cook the beans until tender but still firm. Drain well and immediately pour the marinade over the beans while they are still hot. Cover the bowl and refrigerate.
3. Serve on a bed of leaf lettuce. Garnish with wedges of egg white, half circles of red pepper, spicy Greek olives, and/or tomato wedges.

4 SERVINGS

Lemonnaise Green

If you want a mayo that's a little different, try this one. Serve over tossed salads, coleslaw, or even as a dip for raw vegetables. The first half of the recipe will stand alone if you don't want to bother with the green part.

LEMONNAISE

- 1 egg white
- ½ teaspoon dry mustard
- ½ teaspoon sugar
- ⅛ teaspoon salt
- 1 cup canola oil
- Juice of ½ lemon (about 1½ tablespoons)
- ½ tablespoon hot water

1. In a food processor or blender, combine the egg white, mustard, sugar, and salt. Blend until the mixture is a little frothy.
2. With the food processor still running, gradually add half the oil, pouring in a thin stream. Slowly add 1 tablespoon of the lemon juice.
3. With the processor running again, dribble in the rest of the oil and lemon juice. Add the hot water and continue to mix until thoroughly blended. The mixture can be used at once or refrigerated.

ABOUT 1 CUP

GREEN INGREDIENTS

    4–6 broccoli florets, cooked (about ¼ cup)
    ⅓ pound kale, cooked (¼ cup)
    1 tablespoon chopped fresh parsley
    1 tablespoon snipped fresh chives
    1 teaspoon chopped fresh tarragon
    1 teaspoon chopped fresh chervil
    1 teaspoon snipped fresh dill
    ¾ cup Lemonnaise
    Salt and freshly ground pepper

1. In a food processor or blender, combine the broccoli and kale with the herbs and blend until smooth.
2. Add the Lemonnaise and the salt and pepper to taste and blend again until well mixed.
3. Place in a glass or plastic container and chill for at least 2 hours before using.

Rosemary Tarragon Vinegar

Sprigs of these two herbs are visually intriguing when bottled up together — and their flavors mesh. For the best results, seek out white wine or champagne vinegar.

> *3 large sprigs rosemary*
> *3 large sprigs tarragon*
> *2 cups white wine or champagne vinegar*

1. Put the herbs into a pint bottle and pour in the vinegar (or divide the ingredients between two smaller bottles). Use sterilized glass bottles.
2. Seal nonmetallic lids with hot paraffin wax. Store for 2 to 3 weeks before using.

1 PINT

Thyme, Lemon Peel, and Black Pepper Vinegar

With spirals of lemon peel climbing inside the bottles, this vinegar makes a pretty gift. The addition of 2 or 3 hot dried red peppers will radically change its personality.

3 large sprigs fresh thyme
1 long spiral lemon peel
2 heaping teaspoons black peppercorns
2 cups white wine vinegar

1. Put the thyme, lemon peel, and peppercorns into a pint bottle or two 8-ounce bottles. Use sterilized glass bottles. Add the wine vinegar. Seal nonmetallic lids with hot paraffin wax.
2. Store for a month or so before using, and remember to give the bottles a gentle shake every day or two to keep the peppercorns moving. You could also add the dried concoction called pickling spice to this vinegar for quite a different effect.

1 PINT

Creamy Herb Salad Dressing

With mustard, a mixture of herbs, and the tang of capers, this dressing puts zing into a salad of crisp, mixed greens. It will also go with vegetables that have been cooked for a few minutes and chilled: snow peas, for instance, or green beans or tiny florets of broccoli.

HINT: If you only occasionally use buttermilk, look for the powdered variety, which can be stored on a shelf. You will always have buttermilk at hand in any quantity.

⅔ cup sour cream or yogurt
½ cup buttermilk
2 tablespoons minced capers
2 tablespoons minced fresh parsley
2 teaspoons snipped fresh dill
2 teaspoons minced fresh basil leaves
1 garlic clove, minced
1 teaspoon dry mustard
1 tablespoon lemon juice
¼ teaspoon celery seeds
Salt and freshly ground pepper

1. Whisk together the sour cream or yogurt, buttermilk, capers, parsley, dill, basil, garlic, mustard, lemon juice, celery seeds, and salt and pepper to taste. Let stand for at least 30 minutes so the flavors will blend.
2. Combine with a salad. Preparation time is about 15 minutes.

1½ CUPS

Garlic Mayonnaise

It's not hard to make mayonnaise, and it's quite a nice change from what comes in a commercial jar. Here's one spiked with garlic.

> 2 egg yolks
> Juice of one medium lemon (about 3 tablespoons)
> 4 to 5 garlic cloves, minced
> 2 teaspoons minced fresh parsley
> 1 tablespoon minced shallots
> 2 teaspoons Dijon mustard
> ¾ teaspoon salt
> Freshly ground pepper
> ½ cup extra virgin olive oil

1. In a blender or food processor, combine the egg yolks, lemon juice, garlic, parsley, shallots, mustard, salt, and pepper to taste. Blend until smooth.
2. With the blender still going, pour in the oil in a thin stream. The mayonnaise will thicken as the oil is poured in.

¾ CUP

Ensalada de Naranjas

The sweetness of navel oranges and the crispness of cucumbers put fruit and vegetables in happy combination in this traditional Mexican salad.

> 1 head curly endive or approximately 12 ounces
>   fresh spinach
> 3 navel oranges, peeled and cut into thin slices
> 1 large cucumber, unpeeled, sliced very thin
> 1 tablespoon finely chopped fresh oregano
> 3 scallions, cut into ¼-inch pieces
> ¼ cup olive oil
> ½ cup vinegar
> Freshly ground black pepper

1. Arrange the washed and drained endive or spinach in a shallow bowl.
2. Place the orange and cucumber slices in a decorative pattern over the greens. Sprinkle the oregano and scallions on top.
3. Mix the oil, vinegar, and pepper to taste and pour over the salad.

4 SERVINGS

Crisp Apple Salad with Cheese

The traditional Waldorf salad with apples, chopped walnuts, and mayonnaise has been a staple at cafeterias for decades. This apple salad has a whole new taste and will be especially good in the fall when apples have just been picked and are at their crunchy best.

BALSAMIC VINAIGRETTE
⅓ cup extra virgin olive oil
2 tablespoons balsamic vinegar
Salt and freshly ground pepper
1 garlic clove, cut in half lengthwise with green
core removed

1. Combine the oil, vinegar, salt and pepper to taste, and garlic in a small jar with a lid. Shake and let stand for at least 15 minutes, or leave in the refrigerator for a day.
2. Remove the garlic and use within 2 days.

The salad

    2 Cortland apples, unpeeled, cored, and thinly sliced
        in wedges or circles
    1 cup diced fennel bulb
    1 tablespoon minced fresh parsley
    Balsamic vinaigrette
    2 cups torn Boston lettuce
    2 cups torn romaine
    1 cup torn red or green oak leaf lettuce
    1 cup torn arugula
    ⅓ cup crumbled blue cheese
    Fennel leaves for garnish

1. Put the apples — Cortlands are recommended because they stay white after they are cut, but other varieties may be used if you prefer — and the fennel in a large salad bowl. Toss with the parsley and the balsamic vinaigrette.
2. Layer the various lettuces on top. Cover with plastic wrap and refrigerate. The salad may be made 2 or 3 hours ahead of time.
3. When it is time for dinner, sprinkle the crumbled cheese on top and toss lightly. Garnish with a few fennel leaves.

8 SERVINGS

Sweet cicely represents gladness.

Raspberries with Chevre

A smooth-textured, well-made chevre (goat cheese) has a slight sharpness that
combines well with the flavor of fresh raspberries in this pretty green, white,
and red salad.

SALAD
   1 *head curly endive or red-leaf lettuce, freshly washed and dried*
   ½ *cup chevre*
   1 *cup raspberries*

DRESSING
   1 *teaspoon honey*
   Pinch of dry mustard
   1 *tablespoon white wine vinegar*
   3 *tablespoons safflower oil*
   1 *tablespoon sweet cicely*

1. Tear the endive or red-leaf lettuce into attractive beds and cut the chevre
   into small pieces.
2. Arrange on a plate with the raspberries.
3. Whisk together the honey, mustard, vinegar, oil, and sweet cicely. Pour the
   dressing over the salad and toss gently.

4 SERVINGS

Mint Dressing for Fruit

A fruit salad is festive on a buffet table at any time of the year. Choose fruits that are in season and nicely ripened. They should be carefully washed, peeled, and sliced, then placed in a handsome bowl.

> ½ cup granulated sugar
> 1½ cups vegetable oil
> Juice of 5 large lemons (about 1 cup)
> 1½ teaspoons salt
> An 8-inch sprig of fresh mint leaves

1. Place the sugar, oil, lemon juice, salt, and mint in a blender. Blend until smooth.
2. Pour into a glass container, cover, and refrigerate at least 12 hours. Dribble over fruit.

3 CUPS

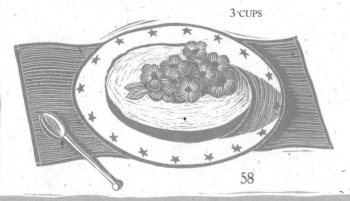

Minted Melon with Violets

A honey dressing spiked with mint makes a delicious dressing for cantaloupe. Violets add a little glamour. If they've stopped blooming, substitute pansies or Johnny-jump-ups, preferably in shades of purple.

> 2 tablespoons honey
> ⅔ cup water
> 1 mint sprig
> ⅔ cup apple juice
> 1 tablespoon lemon juice
> 2 tablespoons chopped applemint
> 2 small cantaloupes
> Violets for garnish

1. Gently heat the honey in the water until it dissolves. Bring to a boil, add the mint sprig, and simmer about 10 minutes. Cool and remove the mint.
2. Combine the liquid with the apple juice and lemon juice. Add the chopped applemint.
3. Slice the cantaloupes across (not lengthwise) into 3 (1-inch) circles and remove the seeds from the center. Peel the rings. Place a ring on each salad plate and pour some of the dressing into each. Decorate with chopped and whole violets.

6 SERVINGS

Stuffed Nasturtiums

Nasturtiums not only tumble out of window boxes with a profusion of round green leaves and orange, coral pink, or yellow blossoms but also can come to the table with quite an elegant display of manners.

8 ounces cream cheese
3 tablespoons mayonnaise
¼ cup chopped nuts
1 carrot, grated (about ¼ cup)
1 tablespoon finely minced green pepper
2 teaspoons chopped fresh basil, parsley, dill, or
   other herb
1½ dozen brilliant nasturtium blossoms, washed
Chives for garnish

1. Soften the cream cheese with the mayonnaise. Add the other ingredients, except for the nasturtiums.
2. Roll the mixture into balls and fit into the nasturtium flowers. Top with a bit of chives or any other edible blossom.
3. Ring a platter with round, bright green nasturtium leaves and arrange the stuffed flowers in the center. These could also be served individually as an hors d'oeuvre.

6 SERVINGS

Dill was once considered a magical herb
that could ward off witchcraft.

Index

Converting Recipe Measurements to Metric

Use the following formulas for converting U.S. measurements to metric. Since the conversions are not exact, it's important to convert the measurements for all of the ingredients to maintain the same proportions as the original recipe.

When The Measurement Given Is	Multiply It By	To Convert To
teaspoons	4.93	milliliters
tablespoons	14.79	milliliters
fluid ounces	29.57	milliliters
cups (liquid)	236.59	milliliters
cups (liquid)	.236	liters
cups (dry)	275.31	milliliters
cups (dry)	.275	liters
pints (liquid)	473.18	milliliters
pints (liquid)	.473	liters
pints (dry)	550.61	milliliters
pints (dry)	.551	liters
quarts (liquid)	946.36	milliliters
quarts (liquid)	.946	liters
quarts (dry)	1101.22	milliliters
quarts (dry)	1.101	liters
gallons	3.785	liters
ounces	28.35	grams
pounds	.454	kilograms
inches	2.54	centimeters
degrees Fahrenheit	$5/9$ (temperature − 32)	degrees Celsius

While standard metric measurements for dry ingredients are given as units of mass, U.S. measurements are given as units of volume. Therefore, the conversions listed above for dry ingredients are given in the metric equivalent of volume.